W9-DFM-293

DATE DUE

MARTIN COUNTY LIBRARY SYSTEM, FL

DEMCO 38-296

JUN 3 0 2004

The Science of Living Things

WHAT IS AN ARTHROPOD?

Kathryn Smithyman & Bobbie Kalman

Crabtree Publishing Company

www.crabtreebooks.com

The Science of Living Things Series
A Bobbie Kalman Book

Dedicated by Kathryn Smithyman
For my sister, Jane Davis, for her love and encouragement

Editor-in-Chief
Bobbie Kalman

Editorial director
Niki Walker

Writing team
Kathryn Smithyman
Bobbie Kalman

Editor
Amanda Bishop

Copy editors
Molly Aloian
Rebecca Sjonger

Art director
Robert MacGregor

Design
Margaret Amy Reiach

Production coordinator
Heather Fitzpatrick

Photo researchers
Jaimie Nathan
Laura Hysert

Consultant
Patricia Loesche, Ph.D., Animal Behavior Program, Department of Psychology, University of Washington

Photographs
Frank S. Balthis: page 30
Robert McCaw: pages 6 (top), 24
McDonald Wildlife Photography, Inc.: Joe McDonald: pages 9, 14, 18 (bottom), 22 (bottom)
Diane Payton Majumdar: page 25 (top)
Allen Blake Sheldon: pages 11 (top), 18 (top), 21 (top and middle), 26
Tom Stack & Associates: Jeff Foott: pages 6 (bottom), 7 (bottom right); John Gerlach: page 1; Joe McDonald: page 28; Milton Rand: pages 11 (bottom), 27 (bottom); Mike Severns: page 21 (bottom); Tom and Therisa Stack: pages 19, 27 (top); Ryan C. Taylor: page 17
Michael Turco: pages 12, 22 (top), 29, 31
Other images by Adobe Image Library, Digital Stock, and Digital Vision

Illustrations
Barbara Bedell: pages 4 (top left), 5 (harvestman, mite, scorpion, ant, flea, millipede, darkling beetle and ladybird beetle), 8, 10, 12 (top), 15 (bottom), 16 (middle), 17 (top), 22, 24 (top), 29, 31
Margaret Amy Reiach: pages 4 (middle right, bottom left and right), 5 (red-kneed tarantula, trilobite fossil, centipede, and monarch butterfly), 9, 15 (top), 16 (bottom), 20, 21, 24 (bottom)
Bonna Rouse: page 17 (bottom)
Tiffany Wybouw: pages 5 (wasp), 11, 12 (bottom), 19

Crabtree Publishing Company

www.crabtreebooks.com   1-800-387-7650

PMB 16A
350 Fifth Avenue
Suite 3308
New York, NY
10118

612 Welland Avenue
St. Catharines
Ontario
Canada
L2M 5V6

73 Lime Walk
Headington
Oxford
OX3 7AD
United Kingdom

Copyright © **2003 CRABTREE PUBLISHING COMPANY.** All rights reserved. No part of this publication may be reproduced, stored in a retrieval system or be transmitted in any form or by any means, electronic, mechanical, photocopying, recording, or otherwise, without the prior written permission of Crabtree Publishing Company.

Cataloging-in-Publication Data
Smithyman, Kathryn
  What is an arthropod? / Kathryn Smithyman & Bobbie Kalman.
    p. cm. -- (The science of living things series)
This book introduces arthropods, a group of invertebrates which outnumbers all other animal species combined, describing some different types and discussing their physical characteristics, behaviors, and habitats.
  ISBN 0-86505-991-8 (RLB) -- ISBN 0-86505-968-3 (pbk.)
  1. Arthropoda--Juvenile literature. [1. Arthropods.] I. Kalman, Bobbie. II. Title. III. Science of living things
  QL434.15 .S54 2003
  595--dc21

LC 2002012123

Contents

What is an arthropod? 4

Arthropod bodies 6

Crustaceans 8

Arachnids 10

Insects 12

Other arthropods 14

Growing from eggs 16

Molting 18

All kinds of change 20

Getting some air 22

Living on plants 24

Feeding time 26

Arthropod defenses 28

Dangers to arthropods 30

Glossary and Index 32

What is an arthropod?

Arthropods are animals. They are **invertebrates**, which means they do not have backbones. Unlike other invertebrates, such as worms and mollusks, arthropods have at least six legs, and their bodies are covered in hard cases called **exoskeletons**.

There are more arthropods on Earth than all other kinds of animals put together! There are well over a million known **species**, or types, of arthropods, including all kinds of insects, spiders, scorpions, lobsters, and crabs. Scientists think there may be thousands, or even millions, of species that have not yet been discovered! To make arthropods easier to study, scientists divide them into **subgroups**, or divisions, as shown on these pages. The arthropods in a subgroup have similar bodies, but they do not all look alike.

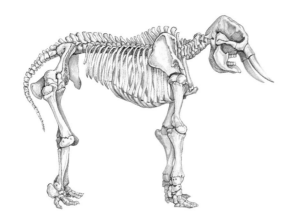

Vertebrates are animals that have **spinal columns**, or backbones. Fish, birds, reptiles, mammals, and amphibians are vertebrates. The skeleton shown above is that of an elephant.

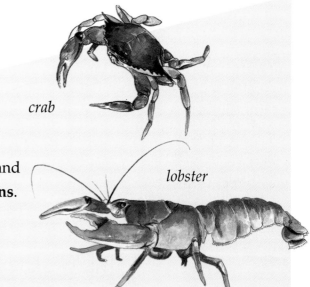

crab

lobster

shrimp

Crustacea

Shrimps, lobsters, and crabs are **crustaceans**. Most live in salt water, but a few live in fresh water.

Chelicerata

The arthropods in this subgroup are named for their special mouthparts, called **chelicerae**. Most are **arachnids**, which include spiders, scorpions, mites, and ticks.

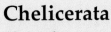

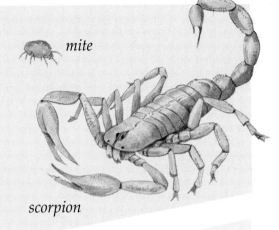

mite

scorpion

harvestman

red-kneed
tarantula

trilobite fossil

Trilobita

Arthropods called **trilobites** make up this subgroup. They became **extinct**, or disappeared from Earth, about 250 million years ago.

Uniramia

Uniramia includes insects, millipedes, and centipedes. It contains more species than all the other subgroups combined.

ant

wasp

flea

ladybird beetle

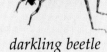

darkling beetle

millipede

centipede

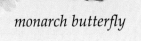

monarch butterfly

Arthropod bodies

No matter how arthropods may differ from one another, their bodies share some common traits. An arthropod's body is made up of many **segments**, or small parts, that are joined together. Every arthropod has an exoskeleton that protects the soft body parts of the animal. In order to move around, an arthropod has jointed **appendages** such as a tail and legs. It can bend its appendages wherever there is a joint. In fact, the word "arthropod" means "hinged feet."

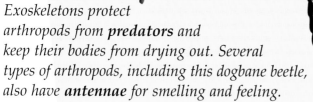

*Exoskeletons protect arthropods from **predators** and keep their bodies from drying out. Several types of arthropods, including this dogbane beetle, also have **antennae** for smelling and feeling.*

On the move

An exoskeleton is made up of many plates, like a suit of armor. These plates help the arthropod move more easily. This sand dune cricket also has bristles on its feet. The bristles grip the sand and help the cricket move.

Segmented bodies

Arthropod bodies may not have the same shapes, or even the same parts, but they are all made up of segments. The segments join together to form two or three main sections. Insects have three sections—a head, a **thorax**, and an **abdomen**. Spiders, scorpions, mites, millipedes, centipedes, and all crustaceans have two main body sections—an abdomen and a **cephalothorax**. A cephalothorax is a fused head and thorax.

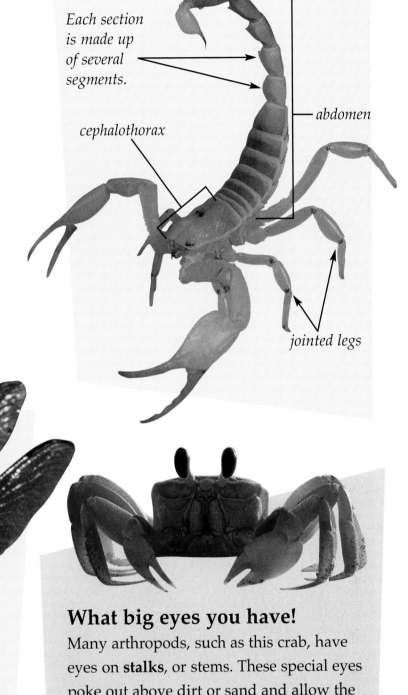

Each section is made up of several segments.

cephalothorax

abdomen

jointed legs

*Many arthropods—especially flying insects—have **compound eyes**, which have many lenses for detecting motion.*

head

thorax

abdomen

What big eyes you have!

Many arthropods, such as this crab, have eyes on **stalks**, or stems. These special eyes poke out above dirt or sand and allow the animals to see what is happening around them while they are hiding at the bottom of the ocean or under the ground.

Crustaceans

Crustaceans have two main body sections, at least five pairs of legs, and two pairs of antennae. There are nearly 40,000 species of crustaceans, which include shrimps, lobsters, crabs, and barnacles. Some crustaceans are so tiny that they can be seen only with a microscope, whereas others are the size of small cats!

Unlike other arthropods, most crustaceans live in water. Some, such as lobsters and crabs, are **bottom-dwellers**. They crawl over ocean floors and lake bottoms. Other crustaceans swim or float near the water's surface. A few types of crabs spend most of their time on land, but they return to water to **reproduce**, or make babies.

This sheep crab gets its name because a layer of algae covers its exoskeleton and makes it look woolly.

Barnacles

Barnacles are crustaceans that cannot move from place to place, even though they have legs. A barnacle starts its life as a soft tiny **larva** (see pages 20-21). It floats until it finds a hard object, attaches itself to the surface, and then grows an exoskeleton. From then on, the barnacle is locked to its spot. It grows long, feathery legs that wave in the water and trap bits of food that float by.

This crab has two barnacles attached to its shell.

Tiny crustaceans

Millions of tiny crustaceans, including krill, live in huge groups near the ocean's surface. They are called **zooplankton**. Zooplankton live amid **microscopic** plants and other tiny animals and feed on specks of algae. Many large sea animals, including whales, feed on krill. Blue whales eat up to 5,500 pounds (2500 kg) of krill a day.

9

 # Arachnids

Arachnids have two body sections, eight legs, and no antennae. There are at least 40,000 species of arachnids, including all kinds of mites, ticks, scorpions, spiders, and harvestmen. The smallest arachnids are microscopic. The longest arachnid is the South African rock scorpion, which is eight inches (21 cm) long.

A few spiders live on water, and some mites live in water, but most arachnids live on land. Spiders, harvestmen, mites, and ticks are found almost everywhere in the world. Scorpions live mainly in warm areas. Most arachnids are **solitary**, or live alone. They usually do not travel far from their homes.

Slurp!

Arachnids do not have jaws, so they cannot chew their food. Some mites are **parasites**. Parasites live on or in the bodies of **hosts**, or other animals, and feed off them. A few types of arachnids, including harvestmen and most mites, are able to eat tiny pieces of food, but most suck up their food through their chelicerae. Spiders and scorpions shoot digestive juices into or onto their **prey**. The juices turn the prey's soft body parts to liquid, which is then sucked up by the spider or scorpion.

*A scorpion has a stinger on the end of its tail. The stinger contains **venom**, or poison. The scorpion uses its stinger to kill prey and to defend itself against attackers.*

A harvestman, or daddy longlegs, is not a spider! Its body sections are joined by a wide waist, whereas a spider has a narrow waist.

Arachnid facts:

- Most arachnids are solitary, but some spiders live together on huge **community webs**.

- To travel long distances, baby spiders and mites **balloon**, or let the wind carry them.

- Harvestmen are predators, but they also feed on fruit juices and some plants.

- Scorpions are **nocturnal**, which means they are active at night. They spend the day hiding in burrows, under rocks, and in the deep cracks of rocks.

Insects

About three quarters of the animals on Earth are insects! There are more than a million known species of insects, and scientists discover about 10,000 more every year. All types of flies, beetles, ants, butterflies, moths, bees, mantises, grasshoppers, stick insects, wasps, and cockroaches are insects.

Insects are found almost everywhere, from deserts to rainforests to the Arctic. Many insects live in **leaf litter** and soil. Others live on plants or under the bark of trees. Some insects are suited to living in swamps, ponds, lakes, and other freshwater areas. areas. A few species live in salt water.

There are more types of beetles in the world than any other type of insect. There are 35,000 species of scarab beetles alone! The beetle in this photograph is a silver scarab.

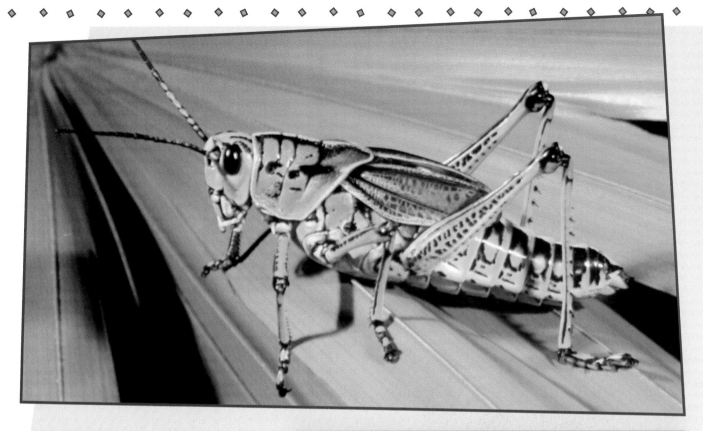

Different insects

All insects have three body sections, six legs, and a pair of antennae. Most also have wings attached to their thoraxes. On some insects, a pair of small wings is joined to a larger pair. The two wings make up one large wing on each side of the insect's body.

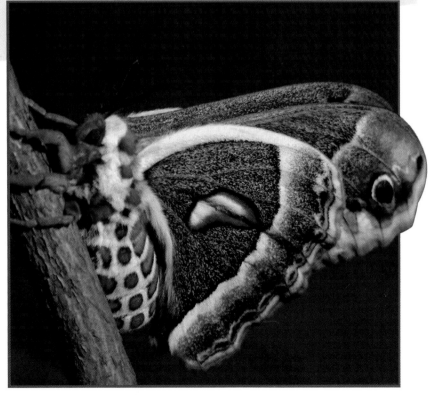

The beetle (left) has the same basic body structure as that of every other insect, including the grasshopper (above) and the moth (right).

Other arthropods

It is not easy for scientists to group the millions of species of arthropods into categories. In fact, they have reorganized the subgroups several times! Each of the three subgroups contains some arthropods that do not seem to fit. For example, horseshoe crabs are not crustaceans but belong instead to the Chelicerata subgroup.

Their bodies are more like those of spiders than those of crabs. Like spiders, horseshoe crabs lack both antennae and jaws. They are an ancient species. Horseshoe crabs have been on Earth for more than 200 million years! In that time, their bodies have changed very little. Learn more about horseshoe crabs on the Internet at www.audubon.org.

In late May, thousands of horseshoe crabs crawl out of the ocean to lay eggs on the shore of Delaware Bay in Maryland, USA. Another population of horseshoe crabs lives in Japan.

Centipedes

There are about 2,800 kinds of centipedes. They all have flat bodies with a pair of legs attached to each of their body segments. Most centipedes are predators. They feed on worms, slugs, spiders, and other centipedes. Centipedes are able to move quickly to catch their prey, which they paralyze with venom. The venom is found in claws on either side of their mouths. Most centipedes live in holes in logs and are nocturnal.

The Uniramia subgroup contains both centipedes and millipedes. They are grouped together with insects since they have three body sections. Their bodies are made up of many segments.

Millipedes

The word "millipede" means "a thousand feet," but millipedes do not actually have a thousand feet! They have two pairs of legs attached to each of their body segments. Having so many legs does not help millipedes move quickly. In fact, it slows them down. Millipedes do not need to move quickly because they are not hunters. Their legs help them tunnel through soil, where they feed on rotting leaves and wood.

Growing from eggs

Male and female arthropods of the same species **mate** in order to produce offspring. Most females then lay hundreds of eggs. After a time, baby arthropods hatch from the eggs.

Arthropod eggs

Arthropod eggs must stay moist. Many insects, including most species of flies, lay their eggs on or near water. Other arthropods do not lay their eggs in water, but they keep them moist in other ways. Spiders, for example, wrap their eggs in coverings called **egg sacs** to keep the eggs from drying out. Egg sacs also help protect the tiny spider eggs from predators.

egg sac

On their own

Most arthropods do not guard their eggs. Females usually lay their eggs and then leave them on their own. They often hide the eggs, however, so predators will not find them. Many females lay their eggs among leaves.

Hatching inside

A scorpion carries her eggs inside her body instead of laying them, as other arthropods do. The babies hatch inside her body and then crawl out onto her back, where they stay until they go off on their own.

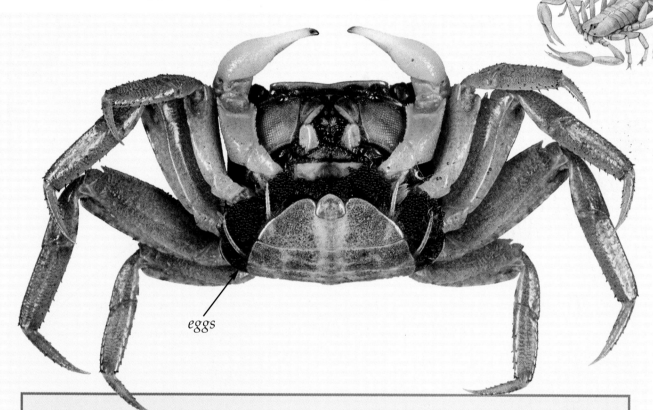

eggs

Egg watchers

A few types of arthropods, such as crabs, guard their eggs until the eggs hatch. The female fiddler crab, shown above, carries her eggs in a special opening in her exoskeleton.

Arthropods such as termites, ants, and bees live in **colonies**, or groups, and work together to watch over eggs. They care for the eggs of every group member and for the newly hatched young.

Molting

As an arthropod grows, its exoskeleton does not stretch along with its body. When its case becomes too tight, the arthropod must **molt**, or shed, it. A soft new exoskeleton is waiting underneath the old one. It takes some time for the arthropod's new covering to dry and harden. While the arthropod waits, it makes its body swell, creating extra growing room in its new exoskeleton.

The exoskeleton above was shed by a crayfish. The crayfish below has to wait until its new exoskeleton hardens before it can scuttle away.

Exposed to danger

Molting is a dangerous time. Without its hard case, an arthropod's soft body can be damaged or eaten by predators. A molt can take from several minutes to a whole day to complete. An arthropod cannot move, eat, or defend itself until its new exoskeleton is dry and firm. The red-kneed tarantula, shown below, is helpless until its new exoskeleton is ready.

Millions of tiny organisms live in water. Many are parasites that attach themselves to the bodies of underwater arthropods. When the arthropods molt, they get rid of the parasites along with worn-out exoskeletons.

All kinds of change

Some arthropods look like miniature versions of their parents when they hatch from their eggs. To become adults, they simply grow and molt until their bodies reach adult size. Other arthropods look nothing like their parents when they hatch. They must go through a **metamorphosis** before they become adults. The word "metamorphosis" means "change of **form**," or shape.

*Newly hatched spiders are called **spiderlings**.*

larva

pupa inside a chrysalis

adult beetle emerging from a chrysalis

adult rhinoceros beetle

Complete metamorphosis

Some arthropods go through **complete metamorphosis**—their bodies change totally from the time they hatch to the time they become adults. When these arthropods hatch, they do not look like arthropods at all! For example, insects that hatch as grubs, maggots, and caterpillars eventually become beetles, flies, and butterflies or moths.

When one of these insects hatches, it is called a larva. Before the larva becomes an adult, its body must change completely. The larva encloses itself in a case called a **chrysalis**. The young insect is now a **pupa**. Its body dissolves into a liquid and then becomes a new, different body. When the insect **emerges**, or comes out of the chrysalis, it is an adult with wings and six legs.

Changing in stages

Many types of insects look similar to adults when they hatch, but their bodies are not quite the same as adult bodies. They go through **incomplete metamorphosis** as they grow, which means they change in stages. These arthropods are called **nymphs** when they hatch. A nymph's body changes a little each time it molts. The milkweed bug nymph (above right), for example, does not have wings when it hatches. As it grows, it goes through several molts. With each molt, its body gradually forms wings. When the bug finishes molting, it has become an adult with wings (right).

milkweed bug nymph

adult milkweed bug

Crustacean bodies

Crustaceans also go through incomplete metamorphosis. They go through four stages—egg, **zoea**, **juvenile**, and adult. When a crustacean hatches, it is a tiny creature called a zoea that floats in the water and feeds on microscopic plants and animals. With each molt, its legs and claws develop a little more, and it becomes a juvenile. The juvenile crab (right) will become an adult (left) after several more molts.

Getting some air

spiracles

All animals need oxygen to live. Animals only "breathe," however, if they have lungs that pull fresh air into their bodies and push out used air. Arthropods do not have lungs, but they have other ways of getting air in and out of their bodies. The smallest arthropods simply **absorb**, or soak in, oxygen through their exoskeletons. They are tiny crustaceans called **isopods**, shown above.

Air holes

Insects, centipedes, and millipedes take in air through tiny holes called **spiracles**. They usually have a line of spiracles along the sides of their thoraxes and abdomens. The spiracles are connected to small tubes, called **tracheas**, that carry air. Air enters through the spiracles, and the tracheas carry it throughout the bodies of these arthropods.

Underwater breathing

Water flows into the body of a crustacean through **gills**. The gills draw oxygen out of the water and send it through the animal's body. The gills also release water.

This swamp crayfish has tiny gills at the base of its legs that pull air into the animal's body.

Book lungs

Some Chelicerata take in air through **book lungs**. Book lungs are a series of folds in their exoskeletons. They look like the pages of a book. Air passes between the folds and mixes with the animal's blood, which also moves among the folds. The blood absorbs oxygen and carries it to the rest of the body. Arachnids with book lungs also have tracheas that carry oxygen throughout their bodies.

Most spiders get air through spiracles, but there are a few species that have book lungs instead. All spiders have trachea.

Living on plants

Several types of arthropods feed on plants. Many of the plant-eaters are insects. Bees and butterflies, for example, drink nectar from flowers. Other insects feed on the roots, stems, or leaves of plants. Tiny aphids drink plant juices, caterpillars munch leaves, and termites bore into the bark of trees.

Plant helpers

Although some insects damage or kill plants by feeding on them, many others are helpful to plants. Most flowering plants rely on insects to **pollinate** them so they can make seeds. If plants could not make seeds, they would eventually die out.

Pollen spreaders

Flying insects, such as bees, wasps, and butterflies, travel from flower to flower in search of food. When they land on a flower, pollen rubs onto their bodies. They carry the pollen to other flowers, where it rubs off, causing the flowers to be pollinated. Plants can begin to make seeds after their flowers have been pollinated.

Some bees feed on pollen. This bee has tiny pockets on its legs, which it stuffs with pollen to carry back to its hive.

A link in the chain

Arthropods are part of many **food chains**. A food chain is made up of animals that eat plants and are then eaten by other animals. Energy and nutrients pass along a food chain from one creature to the next. Countless animals, including various types of amphibians, birds, fish, reptiles, and mammals, depend on arthropods for food. Many humans also eat arthropods—especially crustaceans such as crabs, lobsters, and shrimps.

Feeding time

Many arthropods are predators that hunt and eat animals. They feed mainly on other arthropods, including members of their own species! Spiders, scorpions, and insects often catch and eat other insects, spiders, and scorpions. Large arthropods also hunt small birds, mice, frogs, and snakes. The crab spider below captures a wasp that is much larger than itself!

Eating leftovers

Some arthropods are **scavengers**, or animals that feed on dead plants and animals that they find. Most crustaceans are scavengers. They keep the ocean floor clean by feeding on bits of prey that have been left by sharks and other large animals. Some arthropods that live on land are also scavengers.

Finishing the job

A scavenger does not eat every part of a dead animal. After it finishes feeding on the body, there are still nutrients and energy left. They would be wasted if it were not for **decomposers** such as beetles, mites, and maggots.

Clean-up crews

Decomposers break down the leftover body parts such as skin and bones. Some decomposers, such as millipedes, feed on dead plants. As they break down their food, decomposers not only get energy from it, but they also help create a fertile layer of soil called **humus**, which helps plants grow.

Cleaner shrimps are named for their feeding habits. They eat the parasites that live on fish and make them sick. The fish get a cleaning, and the shrimps get a meal!

Millipedes feed on bits of plants in the soil. Their bodies break down these materials and help return the nutrients to the soil.

Arthropod defenses

All arthropods are protected by exoskeletons, but most also have other defenses against predators. Scorpions use venom to fight predators as well as prey (see page 11). Spiders, centipedes, and assassin bugs also have venom. The venom may not kill a predator, but it can stun the attacker long enough for the arthropod to escape. Many arthropods have defenses that help them avoid being attacked. For example, this spiny devil katydid's sharp points can injure enemies that try to grab it.

Blending in

Many arthropods use **camouflage** to defend themselves. Their colors and patterns help them hide. Aphids, grasshoppers, and other plant-eaters are green or brown so they can blend in with the plants on which they live and feed. In order to hide, some arthropods **mimic**, or look like, plant parts. The stick insect, shown right, looks like a twig. A stick insect can also change color to blend in with the plant on which it is sitting.

Other defenses:

 Some crabs and spiders can break off a leg to escape from predators. A new limb begins to form under the animal's exoskeleton but does not appear until it molts again.

 Many arthropods that have brightly colored exoskeletons also taste terrible! Predators avoid eating these arthropods because of their bad taste. Other arthropods have bright colors but do not taste bad. They stay safe by mimicking the bad-tasting arthropods.

Stick insects can be over 14 inches (36 cm) long! Despite their large size, they are difficult to spot when they rest among branches.

Dangers to arthropods

Although arthropods have many types of defenses, they cannot protect themselves against humans. The main threat to arthropods around the world is the same one most animals face—their natural habitats are disappearing. People constantly clear natural areas to make room for cities, industries, and farms. As natural spaces disappear, arthropods have fewer places to live. Pollution is another big problem for arthropods. Crabs, such as the Sally Lightfoot crabs shown above, and other marine arthropods are affected by oil spills and garbage in the oceans and on shore.

Disappearing forests

The world's rainforests are home to millions of species of animals. Many more species have not yet been discovered! People continue to cut down and burn rainforests at an alarming rate, however. Once an area of rainforest is cleared, it does not grow back, and the animals that live there become extinct. Scientists do not know how many arthropod species may be disappearing along with the forests.

Help arthropods

You can help arthropods by learning more about them and about how important they are to our planet. The Internet has great information. Check out these websites:

 www.sasionline.org/arthzoo

 www.earthlife.net/insects

 www.biology4kids.com
(click on "invertebrates")

Glossary

Note: Boldfaced words that are defined in the book may not appear in the glossary.

abdomen An arthropod's rear body section

antennae Feelers that sense motion and scent

appendage A jointed limb, such as a leg, that is attached to the body

camouflage A color pattern on an animal that allows it to hide from enemies

cephalothorax The fused head and upper body of some arthropods

chelicerae Small pincers near the mouth, which are used for biting

compound eye The eye of most insects and some crustaceans, which is made up of thousands of tiny lenses

exoskeleton An arthropod's hard covering

extinct Describing a plant or animal that no longer exists

gill A thin layer of skin on some arthropods through which they take in oxygen from water

juvenile An arthropod that is not yet ready to mate

larva A newly hatched insect

leaf litter On the ground, a layer of decaying plant and animal material, especially leaves

mate To make babies

metamorphosis Stages of change during which an arthropod's body re-forms

microscopic Describing something so small that it can only be seen under a microscope

molt (v) To shed an exoskeleton; (n) the act of molting

pollinate To carry pollen from the flower of one plant to that of another, which allows the plant to make seeds

predator An animal that hunts and kills other animals for food

prey An animal that is eaten by predators

thorax The part of some arthropod bodies to which legs and wings are attached

Index

antennae 6, 8, 13, 14

arachnid 5, 10-11, 16, 19, 23

babies 8, 11, 16, 17, 20, 21

crustacean 4, 7, 8-9, 21, 25, 27

danger 19, 30-31

defense 6, 11, 16, 17, 28-29

egg 14, 16-17, 20, 21

exoskeleton 4, 6, 8, 9, 17, 18, 19, 22, 23, 28, 29

feeding 24, 25, 26-27

insect 4, 5, 7, 12-13, 15, 20, 21, 24, 25, 26, 28, 29

invertebrate 4

metamorphosis 20-21

molt 18-19, 20, 21, 29

parasite 11, 19, 27

pollinate 24, 25

predator 6, 11, 15, 16, 17, 19, 26, 28, 29

thorax 7, 13, 22

venom 11, 15, 28

1 2 3 4 5 6 7 8 9 0   Printed in the U.S.A.   2 1 0 9 8 7 6 5 4 3